How to Set up a Koi Pond:

The History of Koi Ponds..3

Building Your Own Koi Pond..4

   Pond Planning and Design.......................................5

   Preformed vs Liner Ponds 6

   Indoor vs Outdoor Ponds 7

   Laying the Foundation for a Liner Pond 8

   Koi Pond Liners 10

   Pond Technology 14

Plants for the Koi Pond 28

   Floating Plants...30

   Submerged Plants...32

   Emergent Plants 33

Pond Mates for Koi 34

   Goldfish – Carassius auratus 36

   Chinese Hi Fin Banded Shark – Myxocyprinus asiaticus..37

   Apple Snails – Ampullariidae sp.......................38

Wildlife Concerns..38

Ideal Water Parameters & Cycling the Pond......40

Conclusion..43

HOW TO SET UP A KOI POND: THE ULTIMATE GUIDE

Koi ponds are more popular than ever outside their homeland. High quality koi can be found for very low prices nearly anywhere in the world and the setup is not nearly as difficult as you think.

If you've ever dreamed of sitting beside a gentle pool hand-feeding eager koi, then get ready to learn all you need to know on designing and setting up a koi pond!

THE HISTORY OF KOI PONDS

What we call koi in the West are better known as nishikigoi (錦鯉) in their homeland of Japan. Amur Carp (Cyprinus rubrofuscus) are native to the East Asian mainland (Russia, China, Southeast Asia) and have been raised for millennia in stock ponds for food.

However the Japanese raised koi breeding to an art form by selecting for color in their nishikigoi. Koi breeding became popular in the 1820's but was isolated to a small region of the main island of Honshu until the 1910's.

Through their attempts at popularizing the newly industrialized Japan's culture to the rest of the world, koi became a source of national pride and the hobby took off in earnest.

Ornamental carp are an East Asian specialty, much as dog and horse breeding are European one. Goldfish (Carassius auratus) are close relatives to Amur Carp and have been bred in China for almost a thousand years. However Koi are a Japanese specialty and koi ponds are integral to outdoor Kanso, the Nipponese version of feng shui.

BUILDING YOUR OWN KOI POND

This section covers everything you need to know about planning and building the perfect Koi pond.

POND PLANNING AND DESIGN

Before you make any purchases you should have a clear idea of how your pond will turn out. While you may make some design tweaks along the way having a solid layout ensures there are fewer surprises once ground has been broken.

Choosing the location is the first step to building a pond. Here are some considerations for the planning stage:

1. Can I see the pond from both inside my home and outdoors?
2. Are the shallows shaded in the summer (in hot climates)? Is it deep enough for overwintering (in cold climates)?
3. Could tree roots potentially penetrate the liner over time?
4. How does my pond fit into my future outdoor building plans?
5. How cohesive is my pond with the rest of my landscape?

Outlining the layout with a spray paint can or series of orange flags will give you an idea of whether the location, size, and shape of your pond is ideal.

PREFORMED VS LINER PONDS

While I'll be talking mostly about liner ponds I wanted to take a moment to discuss the other popular option: using hard plastic preformed ponds.

Made of either pure plastic or a rubberized plastic composite, preformed ponds are a fast, inexpensive way to have an aesthetically pleasing backyard water feature without all of the time-intensive measuring a liner pond requires.

Preformed ponds can be placed into any hole and then filled in around the base. The plastic is also extremely hard and nearly impervious to rocks and roots. However their shape is set when molded and can't be customized or adjusted. Finding just the right design can be a challenge.

Also because they are so rigid they can't be made nearly as large as a liner pond can be. Preformed ponds can even be left above-ground all-year round if you live in a warmer climate, such as Florida or Southern California!

INDOOR VS OUTDOOR PONDS

Pond keepers have quite a few options compared to aquarists, including placing the pond indoors or outdoors. There are several benefits to both choices and you should consider carefully which best suits your goals as a koi pond keeper!

BENEFITS OF AN INDOOR POND

1. Can be enjoyed from a patio or other enclosed space
2. Smaller and typically less expensive
3. Koi can be kept warm all year-round
4. Lack of direct sun prevents algae growth
5. Evaporation easier to manage

BENEFITS OF AN OUTDOOR POND

1. Abundant natural sun for pond plants
2. Backyard fixture
3. Ponds attract wildlife like frogs and dragonflies
4. Fewer concerns over splashing or leaks

LAYING THE FOUNDATION FOR A LINER POND

Once you've decided on the size and location, it's time to start digging! Assuming you aren't working with a landscaping company, some shovels are essential, with pickaxes, maddoxes, and other specialty tools as needed for the soil in your area.

Typically, the first shallow shelf area is 6-12 inches deep, with a main body anywhere from 2 feet or more, depending on your design.

Pond depth is one of the most important aspects of the design because koi have special needs depending on the season. In most temperate countries we get four distinct seasons, including a solid winter.

If your pond freezes over you can overwinter your koi – they enter a state of low activity/suspended animation for the winter. However the pond needs to have an area at least 3-4 feet in depth or it will be too cold for them.

Summers in warmer parts of the country can also be brutal and koi may avoid the shallows where direct sun and dark substrates can send temperatures skyrocketing. You should plan on shade from nearby trees, buildings, or plants like cattails for at least part of the day, as well as some source of moving water to keep oxygen levels high.

Once you've finished the bottom section you'll need a drainage chute for debris and fish waste to collect. When digging, give it a slight bowl-shape to allow gravity and water flow to naturally channel debris here.

Other extras to lay the groundwork for when digging include skimmers, PVC piping, and other buried pond equipment.

I always recommend saving any accumulated soil as well; don't simply toss it about. Extra soil will come in handy for establishing plants, building up waterfalls or embankments, and other landscaping projects!

KOI POND LINERS

Before you start laying the rubber liner you'll first need pond underlayment. This fabric layer provides protection for the all-important liner, cushioning it against sharp rocks, roots, and other leak-inducing hazards.

COLIBROX 15 ft. x 20 ft Geotextile Underlayment

1. High tensile-strength nonwoven polypropylene...
2. Enhances soil stability and controls erosion while...
3. Needle punched nonwoven polypropylene geotextile...

$70.68
Buy on Amazon

Since pond underlayment creates space between the ground and the liner gases from decomposition and other processes can be released. Without underlayment trapped gases can bubble up under the liner, creating a substrate bulge in your pond.

Firestone PondGard 45 Mil 20 x 25-Feet EPDM Pond Liner

1. 20 Year Limited Manufacturers Warranty
2. 45 Mil (1.14 mm) (0.045") EPDM
3. 75 Year Life Expectancy

$394.99
Buy on Amazon

Pond liner itself is quite heavy and you'll need more of it than you think. As long as you aren't using an especially odd-shaped pond, the following calculations will give you enough liner to work with. Remember that you need a bit of overlap on the edges for the liner to continue past the lip of the pond. I recommend around 6-12 inches of extra overlap on each dimension.

1. Maximum pond length + (2x maximum depth) + (2x overlap dimensions) = Pond Liner Length
2. Maximum pond width + (2x maximum depth) + (2x overlap dimensions) = Pond Liner Width

The liner goes directly over the overlayment in a single piece. The amount of underlayment needed follows the same formula.

Note that you can substitute underlayment for a number of alternatives. Any durable fabric can do the trick, even old carpeting. Sand is another popular alternative that provides a solid barrier for the liner but doesn't provide gas flow.

Once your liner is in place, you'll want to place rocks, decorations, and potted plants at strategic areas to secure it in place. Place them both at the bottom, on earthen shelves, and along the overlap at the edges. If you want a bottom substrate, coarse gravel and pebbles are ideal because they allow debris to easily reach the drainage.

You'll also need an additional section of liner if you decide you want to set up a waterfall. This strip runs from the top all the way down into the body of the pond itself.

POND TECHNOLOGY

While the pond appears mostly complete with the hole dug and liner in place, there's still a lot more that needs to be done before we can think about adding fish and plants!

POND FILTRATION

Pond filters come in nearly as much variety as indoor aquarium filters do. From sump to fully biological layouts, there are a lot of ways to filter a pond. Submersible filters are some of the most common. While they aren't as convenient since they work best in the deeper portions of the pond, they are inexpensive and easily customized with the right media!

TetraPond Submersible Flat Box Filter For Ponds Up To 500 Gallons

1. Ideal Filter for Ponds Up to 500 Gallons
2. For clear and healthy water, Fits a wide variety of...
3. Prevents pump from clogging

$20.63
Buy on Amazon

However, if you're working with a bottom drainage or a submerged pump, you can also use a pondside filter. You don't have to get wet working on one and since they sit outside of the pond they can be larger without compromising interior space.

Sale

OASE BioSmart 5000 Pond Filter

1. Innovative Flow-Through filter design with...
2. BioSmart 5000 is suitable for ponds up to 5,000...
3. High-surface area filter foams provide exceptional...

$198.20 −$20.69 $177.51
Buy on Amazon

Typically they also provide distinct zones for each stage of filtration: mechanical, chemical, and biological. Submersible filters are much more limited and typically rely solely on mechanical and chemical means alone, which leaves out nitrifying and denitrifying bacteria.

The only downside is that they are less aesthetically pleasing – however they can be hidden in a side compartment dug into the earth, blocked by plants, or by other creative landscaping means.

POND SKIMMER

One major maintenance issue with outdoor ponds is dealing with all of the debris that can accumulate on and within. Fall leaves, grass clippings, and more can quickly give a pond a cluttered, unpolished look.

Pond skimmers are a recessed housing where the submersible pump resides. Skimmers sit on the edge of the pond and allow water to be pre filtered through a mesh screen before being pumped to the filter or waterfall.

Aquascape 43020 Signature Series 200 Pond Skimmer, Black

1. Provides efficient biological filtration for ponds...
2. Removes unwanted debris from the surface of the...
3. 6 inch weir (opening) and included removable leaf...

$207.98

Buy on Amazon

Without a skimmer you'll need to either be using a net daily to remove debris or risk having pump intakes clog with plant matter. Clogged pumps can overheat in hours, resulting in an expensive replacement issue.

POND DE-ICER

Pond heaters might sound surprising for some folks – after all, isn't the idea that the fish can survive outdoors all year-round? Well, yes, but we have to remember that a pond is an artificial ecosystem. The amount of fish relative to the water volume is much, much greater than any natural pond.

Farm Innovators Model P-418 Premium Cast Aluminum Floating Pond De-Icer, 1,250-Watt

1. Thermostatically Controlled Pond De-Icer Maintains...
2. Constructed Of Patented Cast Aluminum For Ultimate...
3. Fish and plant-friendly heater is for use in ponds...

$47.64

Buy on Amazon

While fish metabolisms are at their slowest in the winter they still consume oxygen. However if your pond has fully iced over the ice caps the surface and prevents gas exchange from happening. If you have too many fish and/or a long winter, they may suffocate before the spring thaw.

De-Icers keep a small hole in the ice open all-year round to ensure oxygen and carbon dioxide can equalize, keeping your fish alive.

If your pond is 2 feet or less in maximum depth and you live in a cold climate, you will need to pick up a proper pond heater. Set it to activate once water temperatures reach 45-50F and check on it a few times a day. A shallow pond can quickly freeze if a power outage or cord gets tripped, killing your koi.

UV STERILIZERS

<u>Algae is a problem</u> for all aquatic ecosystems and ponds are no exception. The more nutrient-rich your water and the more light exposure it gets the more algae will thrive. And since sunlight is by far the best for growing it…You get the idea.

UV sterilizers don't do much for hair and slime algae that grows on rocks beyond killing algal spores. In fact, many pond owners appreciate a light fuzzy green growth on submerged surfaces. However they are perfect for eliminating the free-floating single-celled algae that causes green water blooms.

UV sterilizers also kill most bacteria and the eggs and spores of disease causing parasites like ich and fungi. They require a pump to force water through them but you typically install one along the line running from the main pump to your filter.

If green water is a constant issue, reducing feeding, providing additional shade, and encouraging the growth of competing plants will eliminate nearly all algae issues.

PUMPS AND POWERHEADS

Flow is a major part of the pond technology landscape. We need flow to get water into filters, sterilizers, waterfalls, and other areas of the setup. How many and how powerful your pumps will be depends on the height they have to operate against, the volume of the pond, and their uses.

Sale

VIVOSUN 800GPH Submersible Pump(3000L/H, 24W), Ultra Quiet Water Pump with 10ft High Lift, Fountain...

1. 【Specifications】 Dimensions: 4.1*2.6*3.5inch....
2. 【Detachable & Cleanable】 This profile size...
3. 【Optional Outlet Positions】 Place the pump flat...

$25.95 −$2.96 $22.99
Buy on Amazon

A pump dedicated to running just a fountain or waterfall will be much less powerful than a main filtration pump that also has to force water through a UV sterilizer.

FISH FOOD

Koi food is pretty important because you don't want to feed the same food all-year round.

During the summer months when growth is fastest you should use a more protein-rich formula. Fish meal, shrimp, or some other quality protein source should be the first ingredient.

Sale

Kaytee Koi's Choice Fish Food 10 lb

1. Floating food
2. Provides necessary animal and vegetable proteins
3. Great for koi, goldfish and other pond fish

$28.99 −$15.00 $13.99
Buy on Amazon

During the fall and spring you can switch to a vegetable-based formula. Too much protein goes partially undigested and compounds water quality issues when excreted or left uneaten.

Sale

TetraPond Spring And Fall Diet 3.08 Pounds, Pond Fish Food, For Goldfish And Koi (16469), 3 lb, 7 L

1. COOL-WEATHER POND NUTRITION Transitional diet for...
2. FORMULATED WITH WHEAT GERM Provides a source of...
3. SOFT STICKS Floating sticks are easy for fish to...

$41.49 −$5.50 $35.99
Buy on Amazon

PLANTS FOR THE KOI POND

Pond plants are one of the most exciting aspects to owning a koi pond. They help complete the natural landscape aesthetic, provide food and shelter for your fish, and often flower and reproduce with no effort on your part! I go into much greater detail here on the [13 Most Popular Pond Plants](#) but I'll include some of the most popular here as well!

FLOATING PLANTS

Here are a few floating pond plants that you should consider:

WATER LETTUCE

Water lettuce (Pistia stratiotes) is a popular pond plant. It looks like a floating head of butter lettuce and is incredibly easy to grow. With abundant sun and the nutrient rich waters typical of ponds water lettuce reproduces effortlessly.

Being a tropical species, water lettuce is a bit delicate and can't survive frost. It grows best in USDA zones 10 and warmer.

WATER HYACINTH

Water hyacinth (Eichhornia crassipes) has blooms that resemble terrestrial hyacinth and flowers through most of the summer. The floating bulbs give the plant a unique appearance and they are too tough to be palatable to most herbivorous fish. Since it grows so quickly it also acts as a nutrient sponge, locking away phosphorus and other elements that would feed nuisance algae.

Be responsible with water hyacinth and always throw away or compost any extra in your pond. It is extremely invasive and can drastically upset the balance of natural waterways.

SUBMERGED PLANTS

Here are a few submerged pond plants that you should consider:

HORNWORT

Hornwort (Ceratophyllum demersum) is an excellent choice for koi ponds because you can literally just toss it in and watch it grow. While that's not especially aesthetically pleasing, Hornwort can grow either rooted or free-floating, where it branches out to cover the water's surface.

It grows quickly in even indirect lighting and is great for supplemental oxygenation. Goldfish and koi readily scatter eggs among the dense growth and it's very winter-hardy. Hornwort is also fairly tough and not very palatable to koi.

EMERGENT PLANTS

Here are a few emergent pond plants that you should consider:

POND LILIES

Pond or Water lilies (Nymphaea sp.) just might be the most popular emergent plant for koi ponds. They typically come potted and create the classic lily pad that frogs and fish delight in. Dragonflies rest there and koi find shelter from intense sun and hunting herons.

Pond lilies are easy to grow; the tubers are typically placed in a pot or basket of nutrient-rich mud. Every other year or so, adding root fertilizer tab sensures the lilies have enough nutrition to put out leaves and brilliant blossoms.

POND MATES FOR KOI

Are you looking for some additional fish to live alongside your koi? Sorry to say, there are few fish that are a good match for koi.

Native game fish like sunfish and bass are tempting as they thrive in the same conditions, however I don't recommend keeping them together. They tend to be far more aggressive, will readily snap up baby koi and goldfish, and can carry parasites that koi aren't as resistant to.

GOLDFISH – CARASSIUS AURATUS

Goldfish are by far the best choice as koi pond mates. They eat the same food, have the same care requirements, and same temperament. Goldfish are typically much smaller than koi but are still sizable.

Keep in mind they will hybridize if left to their own devices, which makes the resulting fry worthless to specialty koi keepers and breeders.

CHINESE HI FIN BANDED SHARK – MYXOCYPRINUS ASIATICUS

These unfortunate fish are typically sold as tropical fish when they are not only temperate but get far too large for indoor aquariums. Usually sold as striped, hunchbacked young with a sail-like dorsal fin, they eventually grow over 4 feet long and lose their bold stripes and showy fins.

Chinese Hi Fin Banded sharks are <u>not sharks</u> – they are cyprinids and thus related to koi, barbs, and goldfish. However they are mostly bottom dwellers, feeding on algae and detritus similar to plecostomus. They are ideal companions for koi in larger ponds and even come from the same part of the world.

APPLE SNAILS – AMPULLARIIDAE SP.

Apple or Mystery snails are a family of large snails that are popular for both aquariums and ponds. They feed on dead and decaying plant matter as well as hair, film, and other nuisance algae growth. Snails are also the perfect detrivore, cleaning up leftover food that gets missed by your koi.

Adult apple snails are too large to be easily eaten by koi but young snails will be swallowed whole. The best way to keep them is to add your snails at the same time as your young koi. The growth of the snails will keep pace with your koi and the koi will keep snail numbers in check as they reproduce.

WILDLIFE CONCERNS

Unfortunately, a shallow lake full of fat, defenseless fish can be a major target for local wildlife. Small koi and goldfish are the most at risk and as they get larger they become too large for all but the most determined predators to eat.

Common Koi Predators include:

1. Neighborhood and feral cats
2. Opossums, raccoons, foxes, and other opportunistic mammals
3. Water snakes, large turtles, bullfrogs
4. Herons, egrets, and other estuarine hunting birds
5. Hawks, eagles, owls, and other birds of prey

Adult koi are too large for even determined herons and eagles to eat. However the birds can still inflict deep puncture wounds that can get infected or even kill. Also beware if you live in rural parts of the world. River otters will delight in taking a soak and hunting down the largest fish for an easy meal.

Deterrents include fences, outdoor pets like dogs, and even decoys to deter herons and egrets, which are by far the worst threat.

Once they find a pond with small koi they'll show up like clockwork at dawn to hunt, leaving you baffled by your koi's disappearing act.

While tacky, floating crocodile heads and fake owls also work, though they need to be moved on occasion to keep the birds from catching on. Floating plants and lily pads also provide cover for fish to hide behind. Darker colored varieties like [Asagi Magoi](#) are also less visible and therefore harder to catch than a brilliant red and white [Kohaku](#).

IDEAL WATER PARAMETERS & CYCLING THE POND

In order to properly cycle the pond, you'll need a water test kit. The best test kits include pH, ammonia, nitrite, and nitrate. I'd also recommend a phosphorus test kit if algae issues are a constant concern but when first setting up your pond it shouldn't be an issue.

Sale

API FRESHWATER MASTER TEST KIT 800-Test Freshwater Aquarium Water Master Test Kit, White, Single

1. Contains one (1) API FRESHWATER MASTER TEST KIT...
2. Helps monitor water quality and prevent invisible...
3. Accurately monitors 5 most vital water parameters...

$35.79 −$12.57 $23.22
Buy on Amazon

There are many ways to start and speed up the cycling process both ponds and aquariums and the methods overlap. I recommend adding a few small fish to create waste for nitrifying bacteria to consume.

Over the course of a few weeks, you can add more fish. Most pond keepers start with a few inexpensive goldfish for cycling. And once your test kits show 0ppm ammonia, low nitrites, and low to moderate nitrate, you know your bacteria are doing their job and have paved the way for your show koi.

While the tried and true method of adding hardy fish to start things off works well, nowadays the bacteria to jump-start the process can be purchased in bulk. By adding nitrifying bacteria directly to the water you can immediately prime the pond to house your koi.

Koi also prefer a pH that's neutral to alkaline (pH 7.0-8.0) and moderate outdoor temperatures of 65-75F in the summer. As temperatures cool in the fall koi stop feeding entirely once water temperatures hit 50F. During the late fall and winter they live off of their stored fat, becoming mostly immobile as their metabolism slows until spring.

CONCLUSION

Koi ponds are a hobby that's centuries old and a fascinating world to break into. From design to stocking, each aspect of the hobby is a delight. And the sheer customizability ensures that even if your neighbors decide to copy you, no two ponds are ever alike!

If you decide to use this information to start your own backyard or indoor pond, give me a shout out and let me know how it goes!

Printed in Great Britain
by Amazon